Tell Me Why

WHY?

We Have Hurricanes

Tamra B. Orr

Published in the United States of America by Cherry Lake Publishing
Ann Arbor, Michigan
www.cherrylakepublishing.com

Content Adviser: Jack Williams, Fellow of the American Meteorological Society
Reading Adviser: Marla Conn, ReadAbility, Inc

Photo Credits: © NASA Goddard Space Flight Center/Flickr Images, 5; © Cheryl Casey/Shutterstock
Images, 7; © behindlens/Shutterstock Images, cover, 1, 9; © Zacarias Pereira da Mata/Shutterstock Images,
11; © Andrey Yurlov/Shutterstock Images, 13; © nico99/Shutterstock Images, 15; © Robert A. Mansker/
Shutterstock Images, cover, 1, 17; © Harvepino/Shutterstock Images, cover, 1, 19;© bluecrayola/Shutterstock
Images, 21

Library of Congress Cataloging-in-Publication Data

CIP data has been filed and is available at catalog.loc.gov.

Cherry Lake Publishing would like to acknowledge the work of the Partnership for 21st Century Skills.
Please visit *www.p21.org* for more information.

Printed in the United States of America
Corporate Graphics

Table of Contents

The Hurricane Hunters 4

Birth of a Hurricane 10

Trouble on Land 14

Future Hunter 18

Think About It! 22

Glossary 23

Find Out More 23

Index 24

About the Author 24

The Hurricane Hunters

"Whoa!" said Kennedy, walking into the kitchen. "That documentary was amazing!"

"What's your new passion this time?" Mom asked.

"It was all about hurricane hunters," he said. "They're people who work for NOAA. That's the National Oceanic and Atmospheric Administration. Hurricane hunters are sent out in planes when a storm nears land. They fly over the ocean and record what is happening. They use this

Hurricane hunters use planes similar to this one to see how a storm is developing.

cool instrument called a **dropsonde**. Have you ever heard of one?"

Mom shook her head.

"The dropsonde is a small tube with a parachute. Hunters drop it into a storm," Kennedy continued. "A **radio transmitter** sends back details to the plane, which radioes the information to weather forecasters. It tells the forecasters if the storm is getting stronger or weaker. The hunters fly through the storms multiple times. They measure temperature, air

WEATHER RECONN

Planes like this one use radio transmitters to send
information to weather forecasters.

pressure, wind speed, and direction. Then they know which way the storm is going and how strong it is."

Kennedy took a deep breath. "Now I have to finish my homework," he said. "After all, you have to get good grades in science and math to be a hurricane hunter."

During hurricanes, the wind and rain get stronger.

Birth of a Hurricane

Kennedy wanted to know more about hurricanes. How did they form? How were they different from **tornadoes** and other big storms? He began reading—and he couldn't stop.

First, Kennedy discovered, hurricanes only form over warm ocean water. The storms are only called hurricanes if they take shape over the Atlantic and the northeastern Pacific Oceans. Over the South Pacific and Indian Oceans, they are called **cyclones**. Over the northwestern Pacific Ocean, they are known as **typhoons**.

Hurricanes can only form over warm ocean water.

All hurricanes begin as **tropical storms**. They need warm water that is 79 degrees Fahrenheit (26 degrees Celsius) or higher to form. As the water **evaporates** into the warm air, the air begins rising. It cools and **condenses** into large clouds. Air over the ocean rushes in to replace the rising air, creating winds. Earth's rotation causes these winds to form a large swirl.

Clouds form when rising warm air cools and starts to condense.

Trouble on Land

"What are you reading that is so interesting?" Kennedy's friend Sam asked.

"Listen to this," Kennedy replied. "Scientists put hurricanes in categories from 1 to 5, from least **destructive** to most. A hurricane at any level will still cause damage to the communities it hits."

"Wow!" Sam said. "That sounds dangerous."

"It can be," Kennedy agreed. "But not many storms reach a 5. This is because when hurricanes hit land, they usually slow down.

MAKE A GUESS!

Hurricane Ike didn't just hit Texas. It also hit Cuba, Haiti, and many other islands. Why do you think the hurricanes that strike islands are often the most dangerous?

The flooding from Hurricane Ike, which hit Texas in 2008, destroyed multiple houses.

That's because they don't have the warm ocean air to feed them. But they're still dangerous. A hurricane pushes a mound of water ashore known as **storm surge**. Heavy rain can move more than 100 miles **inland**, causing floods and **landslides** after the winds stop blowing. Storm surges kill more people than the wind does."

Hurricane Katrina, in 2005, devastated the city of New Orleans.

Future Hunter

"Doesn't a hurricane have an **eye**?" Sam asked. She was right. A hurricane's eye is the calm in the middle of the storm. The eye is usually between 5 and 30 miles (8 and 48 kilometers) wide.

"I want to research hurricanes up close," Kennedy told Sam.

Sam laughed. "I'd join you, but we'll never have one here in Indiana."

Fortunately, only a few parts of the United States are at risk for hurricanes. Most hurricanes in the United States occur on the Gulf Coast and southern Atlantic Coast. In the rest of the world, they tend to strike the Bahamas, West Indies, and Virgin Islands the most.

An earthquake's power is measured by the Richter scale. Hurricanes have the Saffir-Simpson scale. Go online with an adult and learn more about it.

The eye of a hurricane is the calmest part of the storm.

In the north Pacific Ocean, hurricane season starts in May. In the north Atlantic Ocean, it starts in June. By November, the risk has passed.

"I remember hearing about Hurricane Katrina in science class," said Sam. "Why did they call it that? It wasn't the name of the city it hit."

"Each hurricane is given its own name," Kennedy explained. "For years, the National Hurricane Center only used girls' names, and in 1978 they started using boys' names, too."

"I would think so!" Sam said. "That seems fair to me."

Jupiter has had a hurricane blowing for more than 300 years! Through a telescope, it looks like a bright red spot.

Different planets have different weather systems.

Think About It!

Forecasters rate hurricanes in categories based on their wind speed. Hurricane Katrina hit Louisiana as a Category 3 storm. Why was it such a dangerous and costly storm? Go online to find out more.

Almost 90 percent of the people who are killed during hurricanes die due to drowning. How do you think that happens?

Glossary

condenses (kuhn-DENS-iz) reduces to another form, as in a vapor to a liquid

cyclones (SYE-klohnz) storms in the South Pacific and Indian Oceans

destructive (di-STRUHK-tiv) causing damage and harm

dropsonde (DROP-sond) an instrument attached to a parachute and released into a storm from an aircraft

evaporates (ih-VAP-uh-rayts) changes from a liquid or solid state into vapor

eye (EYE) the center of a hurricane where winds are calm

inland (IN-luhnd) located away from the sea

landslides (LAND-slydz) the downward falling or sliding of masses of soil or rocks from steep slopes

radio transmitter (RAY-dee-oh trans-MIT-ur) a device that sends out radio waves with the sounds heard on a radio

storm surge (STORM SURJ) an abnormal rise in the level of the sea along a coast caused by a hurricane or other strong storm

tornadoes (tor-NAY-dohz) windstorms characterized by long, funnel-shaped clouds hanging from the bottom of a thunderstorm

tropical storms (TRAH-pi-kuhl STORMZ) storms that form over a warm ocean with fastest winds between 37 and 63 miles per hour

typhoons (tye-FOONZ) large storms that form over the northwestern Pacific Ocean

Find Out More

Books:

Carson, Mary Kay. *Inside Hurricanes*. New York: Sterling, 2010.

Challoner, Jack. *Hurricane & Tornado*. New York: DK Publishing, 2014.

Web Sites:

National Geographic: Your Shot: #hurricane
http://yourshot.nationalgeographic.com/tags/hurricane/
Look at some amazing photos of hurricanes.

Weather WizKids: Hurricanes
www.weatherwizkids.com/weather-hurricane.htm
See animated images of hurricanes, as well as tips on how to track them.

Index

air, warm, 13
Atlantic Ocean, 10, 20

clouds, 12, 13

dropsonde, 6

flooding, 15, 16

hurricane hunters, 4, 5, 6–8
Hurricane Katrina, 17, 20, 22
hurricanes
    birth of, 10–13
    categories, 14, 22
    eye, 18, 19

measuring, 19
names, 20
season for, 20

islands, 15

Pacific Ocean, 10, 20

rain, 9, 16

storm surge, 16

tropical storms, 12

water, warm, 10, 11, 12, 16
wind, 9, 12, 16

About the Author

Tamra B. Orr is a full-time author living in the Pacific Northwest. She is a mom to four, a graduate of Ball State University, and the author of more than 375 books for readers of all ages. Although she lives in Oregon today, she grew up in northern Indiana and remembers hiding in the basement when tornado warnings were issued. While too far away from water to worry about hurricanes, she can still imagine their incredible power.